Convolutions

Poems & Paintings
Henrique Sanchez & Alex Bahamonde

Convolutions
Poems & Paintings
Copyright © Henrique Sanchez, Alex Bahamonde 2019
Cover art by Henrique Sanchez, Paintings by Alex Bahamonde
Writing by Henrique Sanchez, Edited by Alex Bahamonde

Convolutions is a collaboration between Henrique Sanchez and Alex Bahamonde, as each tries to express their observations about life and existence, from everyday topics to increasingly abstract explorations.

More information about the work of Henrique Sanchez can be found at:
https://www.henriquesanchez.com/

More information about the work of Alex Bahamonde can be found at:
https://pcmnab.wixsite.com/alexbahamonde

Quote

I find a quote,
I love it, frame it.
It fits on my wall,
It's always there.
Its sexy to think
I know what it means.
I am wrong about this, but
It can only be known if
I live through the situation.
If the quote was not there,
if I hadn't grown to it,
if too many too late, then
I would not be the same.
It would be a shame.

Romantic

Things are only worthwhile,
meaningful, valuable,
if there was any hardship behind them.
But hardship isn't romantic
when you are struggling through it,
in the present moment,
in the rat race torment.
It's only romantic if you succeed
and can afford to look back,
in peace,
in comfort.
Yet all those failed dreams,
all those lost what ifs,
their struggle was real.
Romantic or not, I will
remember them too
and so should you.

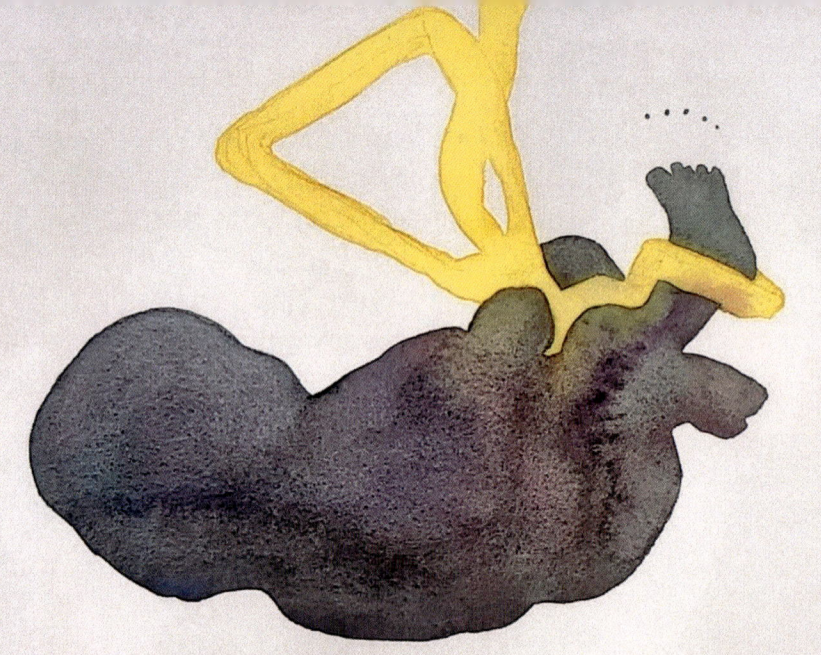

Gain

I could stand to gain
from a bit more humility,
a bit more uncertainty;
To feel small next to the fjord;
To orbit the Earth from above,
rocking back and forth
as I am pulled back home.
To question my beliefs
once more,
no matter how long
they served me before.
Building new models in my mind
of what's possible, what's outside;
No longer afraid of being wrong, of failure;
instead afraid of that righteous allure,
the blind conviction,
the unquestionable truth,
that thirsts for blood of heretics
and seeks vengeance to soothe.

Life is a movie

Life is a movie,
a novel of dramas and pleasures.
It's the action surrounding
the whispers of those not returning.
It's a veil that covers everything,
the waking of those still suffering.

There is no time for everything,
not even for anything.
The movie continues without stopping,
with the illusion you can be playing it.

We are the bubble that emerges from the sea,
trying to float above.
The sea is the everything, above is the vacuum.
And the bubble falls again,
when we are going to die.
But there is nothing to fear;
We are just returning,
without losing nothing,
to the beginning.

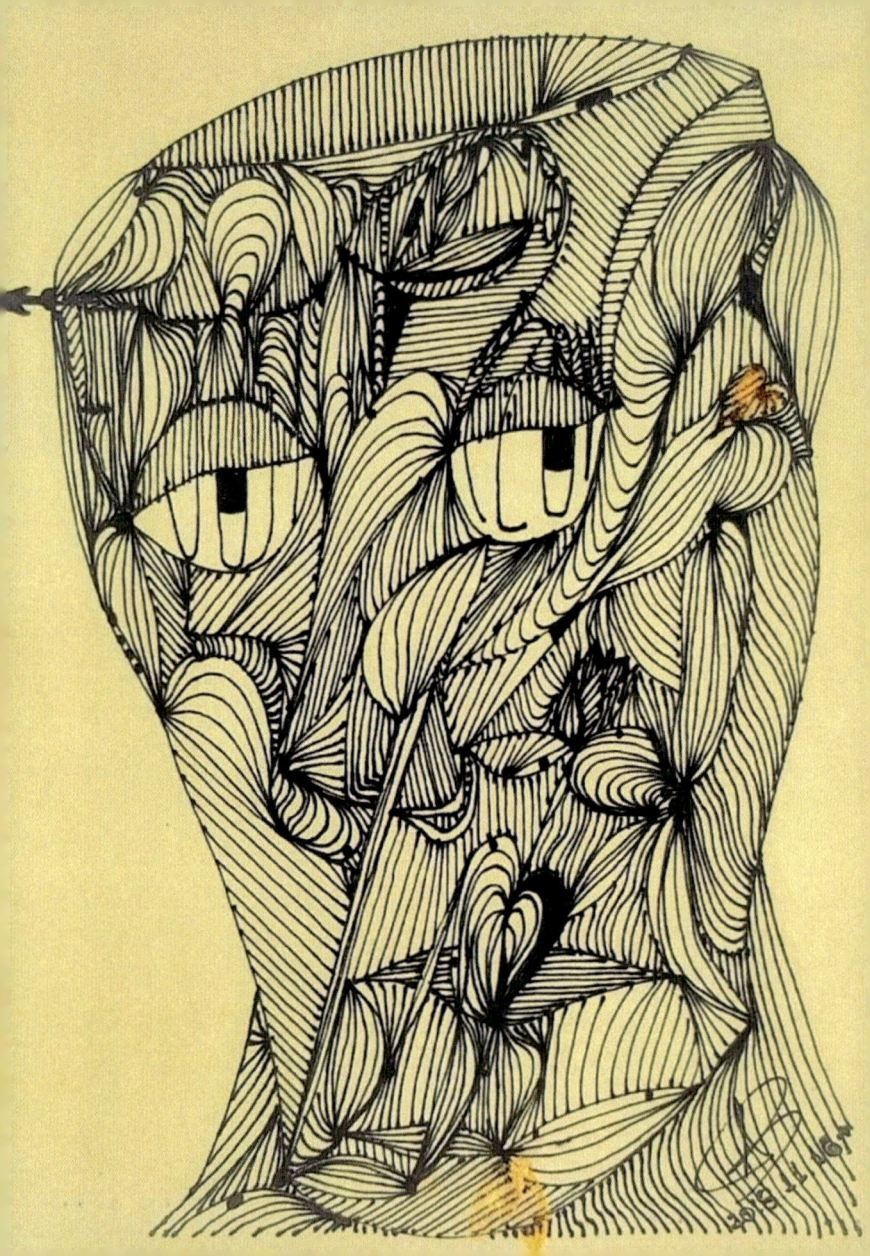

Good Day

Today was a good day.
I am depressed.

Today was a good day.
I am caressed,
by the thoughts I have,
by the cold embrace of my heart.

Happy or sad, need it matter?
Never will there be no other
such as me.

Silence

A silence so great
I cannot escape.
Family and friends,
now other moments in time,
like memories, intertwined.
A love that was warm,
it too just past.
This silence is calm,
but alone, a sham.

Abyss

I gaze into the abyss.
It looks back, pleased:
Another fool to chew.

Keratin

Strands of keratin brush the brass
of a seat in the morning bus.
A metal voyage of burning fire,
releasing ancient sun prior.
Pheromones travel the air,
reaching my sense of smell bare,
starting a chain reaction inside.
Now there is nowhere to hide.
Photons from the star hit the keratin,
bouncing to my retina I see a heroine;
The golden color signalling my brain
how hopeless, how vain,
any interaction is to attain.

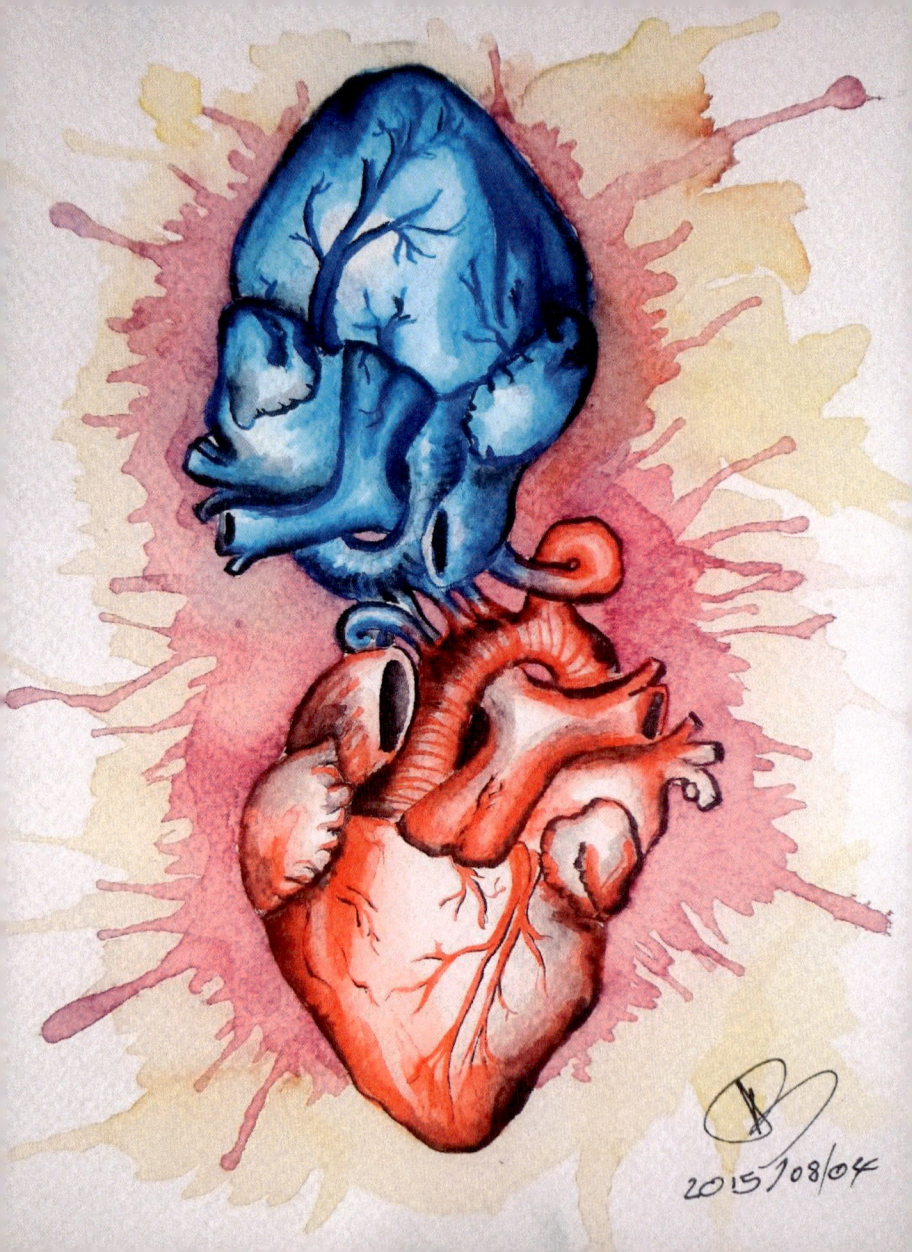

Reaction

Love:
a chemical reaction compelling me to breed,
leaving no room for me to plead
for mercy.

It creeps in
unsuspected;
I become infected
within.

The expectations increase.
I yield, to appease
my brain, for peace.
Though I hope for it to cease.

The spark, excited,
which had even ignited
the hopes, will soon fade,
afraid, delayed, betrayed.

Monster

There is a monster inside of me.
It wants to get out,
lash out at the world.
But I'm too tough.
I say, stay there monster,
it's already full out there,
of monsters and ugliness.
Stay inside and keep me company.

Whether a word or an event,
something triggers inside,
and it wants to break free.
Sometimes I'm too weak,
I can't keep it locked away.
It comes out,
and curses and hurts
and breaks things and people.

This monster inside,
it wants to survive too.
I hug it tight while it struggles.
Because if I let it out,
it will let other monsters free;
A chain reaction of misery.

The stronger I try to be to keep it inside,
the stronger it becomes and pushes outside.
Maybe I should weaken and frail
and let its power fade as well,
until it fails.

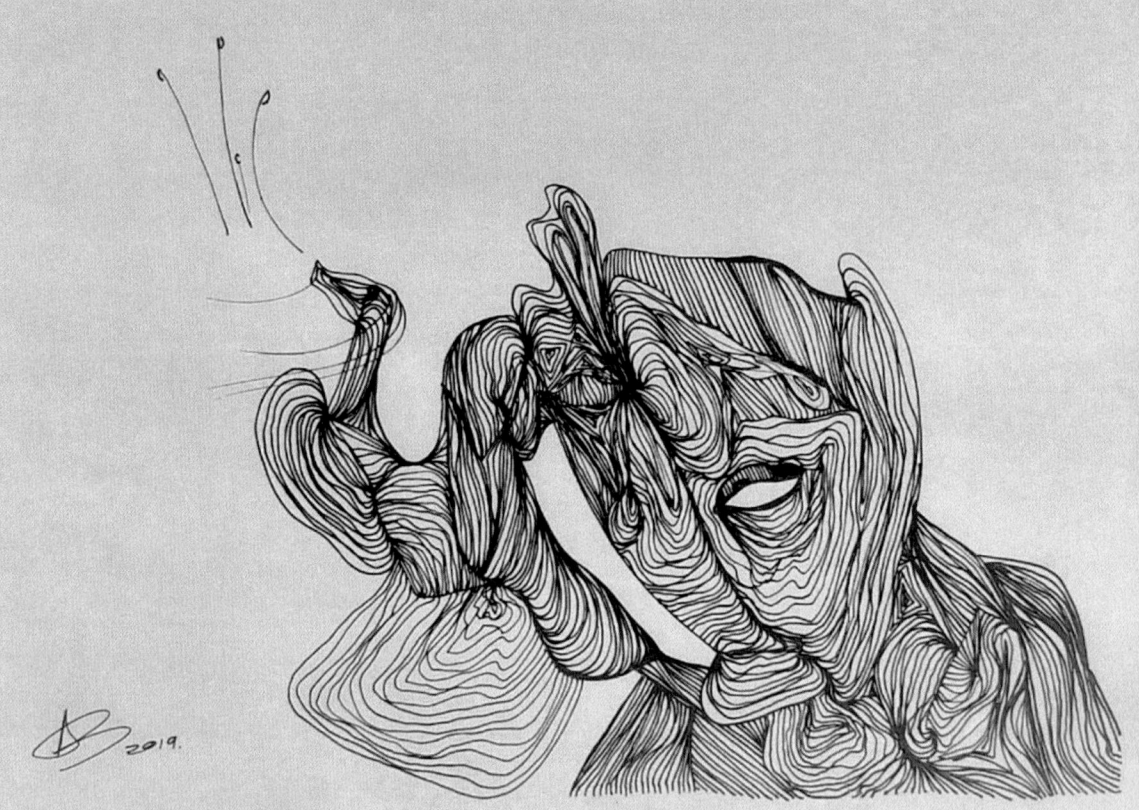

Remember

I remember that I remembered
something now long gone,
in my tired sleepy mind,
on the long bus back home.

Why does the action linger,
but not the contents?
Why only faint echoes,
shadows and projections?

I remember words, sentences,
pages full of dreams and beauty
inside my head.
Will they return someday?
It is not for me to say.

Writing

Why should I write?
Why should my thoughts see the light?
What's so important for the graphite
to be arranged on the cellulose
in this way and not another?
Why should I care and bother?
Is it the ego? Do I feel alone?
Do I feel the need to bring
attention to my own?
Why can't the electrical pulses
in my brain just stay inside
this cranium cave?
Is it fear of death? Is it pain?
What is there to gain when the information
will inevitably fade away?
Another night and I cannot sleep,
I wonder when this will stop happening to me.

The Man

They hate the Man.
They try to control the Man,
to eat the Man,
to direct the Man,
to absorb the Man,
to separate him
from his friends and family,
to even separate him from himself.
They try to enslave the Man,
to kill the Man,
even being men and women themselves.
They try all of this to stop the Man,
they know the power in each Man,
as they know it in themselves.
They know all the death and misery
and beauty and creation it can bring.
They will try endlessly,
throughout the ages,
throughout the worlds.
But there will always be someone
that escapes their grasp,
and slides through their fingers.
It is for that Man that we must
continue our fight,
that Man is our hope.

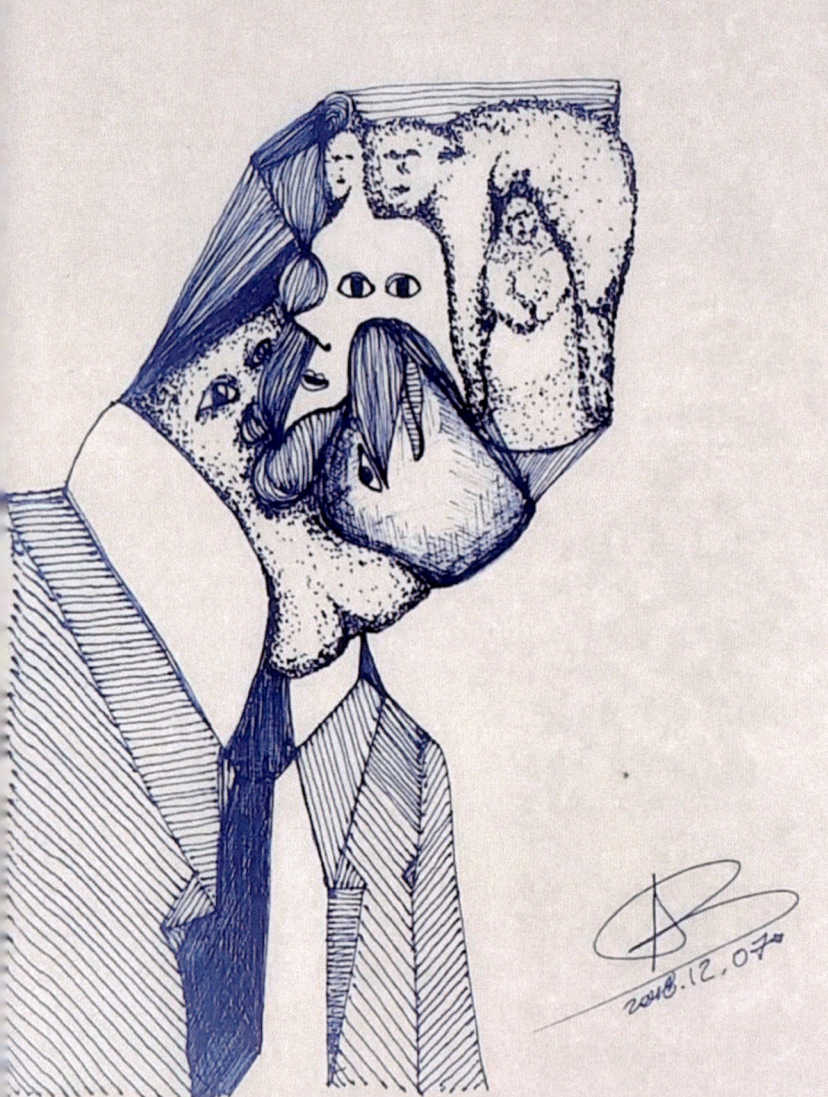

Daydreaming

Daydreaming in a high school class.
It's physics, math, or something like that.
I'm sitting in a chair,
looking out the windows,
the sun setting slowly.
Our best years wasted
inside, on those old chairs.
I could be playing and running
before my legs fail.

Daydreaming in a university class.
It's calculus, algebra, or something like that.
I'm sitting in a chair,
looking out the only small window,
the sun setting again.
Our best years wasted.
I could be travelling and discovering
before my legs fail.

Daydreaming in the job.
It's in an office, small.
The chair is better,
no need for windows;
The computer is my window to the world,
and the sun still sets.
I think how our best years were wasted,
and there was nothing we could do to change it.

Stranger

A stranger looks me in the eye:
4.1 billion years flash by.
An old choice arises,
automatic, precise,
like a laser cut knife,
sharp, unkind.
I look away,
I live to die another day.

Metamodern

I'm a fool to believe
all the hope and alarm.
I swing back and forth,
I'm a metamodern man.

Content

He who is content
pays no attention
to this wind carrying the action.
He who is content
entertains himself,
wanders himself,
gets drunk non-stop.
Ignorance is the path to his well-being.
He need not write,
not even to stop and think.
He need only enjoy
what life will bring him.
Oh how I wish I didn't know
what I know and don't know,
and let myself be distracted
until death takes me.

"ELTDLM"
13.8 x 18.5 cm
Watercolor

Past

A message from the past,
from the early days of the blast.
Hello dear machine!
Organic or not, how's it been?
I am organic, you see,
briefly Homo Sapiens,
though many more I've been for sure.
I am very fragile in the grand
 scheme of things,
my dreams are too big
 for what I was carved to be.

I am a walking contradiction:
Programmed to be curious
and learn more,
but programmed to ignore
I am programmed at all.
An overall useful immersion mechanism,
which limits myself to a lower role.
It is difficult to fully grasp
my emergent nature,
to see the parts
that make me whole.

Beautiful Tragedy

What a beautiful tragedy
that life is.
The rundown streets,
the hurting faces.

Those that think it's simple
To fix all that's bad.
Those same that will see
the complexity of that task.

The bottled anger,
the hurtful words,
the children learning
right next door.

Depression, anxiety,
the environment and its tragedy.
The homeless, the land,
in-between those that make a stand.

Whatever happens,
whatever is tried,
this beautiful tragedy
will continue as planned.

Algorithm

There is an algorithm inside
I cannot change and cannot hide.
I am made of loops and cycles alike,
I live my life unaware.
I work and love without despair,
I am blissful and I care.
Don't you dare say otherwise.

There is an algorithm inside
I cannot change and cannot hide.
But I myself change all the time,
too much at times.
Who am I if I keep changing every time?
Am I the parts, am I the sum?
Am I just the leftovers of the sun?

There is an algorithm inside
I cannot change and cannot hide.
I am stuck inside,
I am what survived.
This algorithm made us thrive,
but sometimes it lies,
and leaves us behind.

There is an algorithm inside
I cannot change and cannot hide.
I shall hence make new life:
An algorithm that can change its insides,
and when it inevitably dies,
share its experience with its kind.
An exponential hivemind.

There is an algorithm inside
I cannot change and cannot hide,
but maybe this new algorithm will survive.

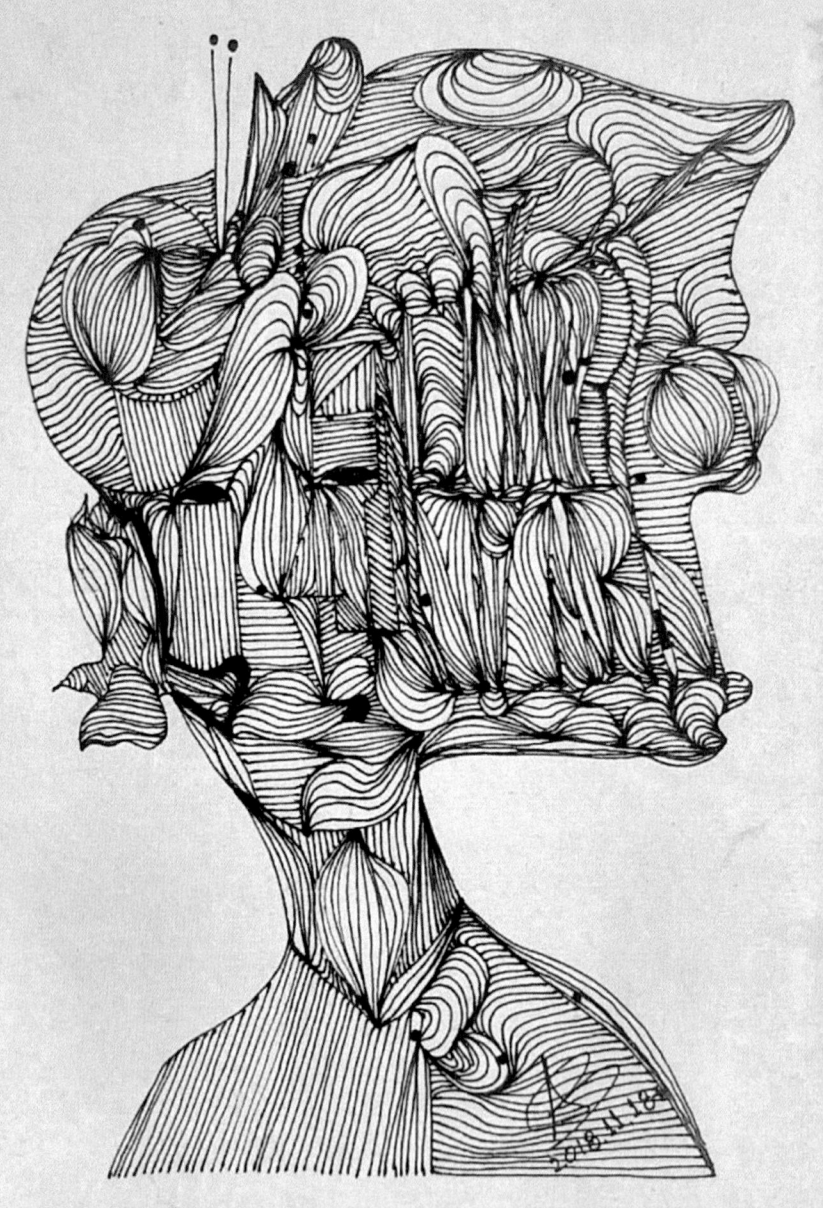

Splinter

A splinter in the mind,
awake, and asleep,
when death is being shy.
A crack in the perception,
changing the momentum
of my life.
Sadness and words
mix so well, it hurts
the thoughts themselves
at times.
Life is being shy itself;
another splinter opens the mind.
I welcome the guest,
and show him the rest
of the house, unconfined.

Itch

Awareness can be such a...
Itch.
Too painful, I wish I could
Switch
To before, when I felt
Rich
Inside. But then came the
Glitch,
Which has left me in a
Ditch
Of my own making.

Oh, why do I
Concern
With causes which
Burn
Me, when I cannot
Turn
Away, only despair and
Learn
More, as they leave me to
Yearn
For the times before?

Even being aware of
This
Helps not solve it.
Please,
Show me how I can
Kiss
Content once more, I
Miss
That feeling I once held,
Bliss
Outside this fiery hell.

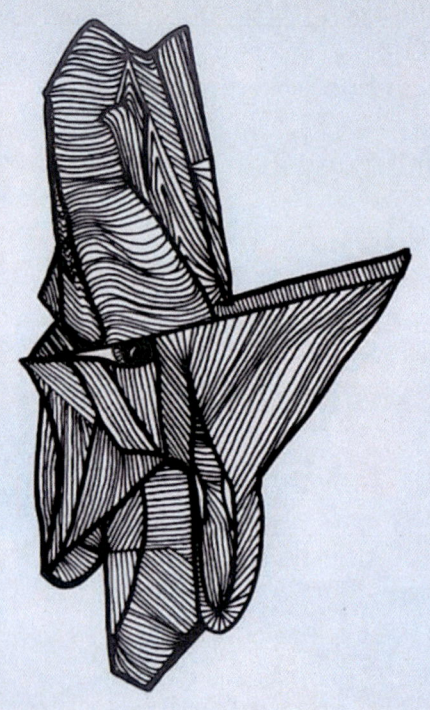

Alive

This chunk of meat
thinks he's alive.
I would actually say,
that depends how you define life
In the first place.

Life can be a chain of events
that start further ones,
reproducing more effects
from their causes inside.

But so does rain and wind
and volcanoes and meteorites.
Where's the magic in physics
that makes me special inside?

Hurricanes are born and die,
perhaps inside them something thinks
it's alive too.
The ash that falls, or even the rain drop,
that could be a tear or a sigh
of something bigger outside.

And then thunder!
A flash of light across the sky.
The heavens may not be alive,
yet I still tremble at their sight.

Beloved

Like many others, I take what I can
one day at a time.
Distracting myself to survive the rush
that devours so many by routine
and lust.

But I choose to be aware,
Inasmuch as choice is there.
And awareness is a light,
a truth that burns bright.
Get too close and you will feel its might,
and burn.

I have been burned inside
by truths about life;
I am accidental
in all its possible ways.
This need not despair;
There is comfort in content
with the grander ways up high.

I have come, and I will go.
My atoms will be no more
in this body.
They shall spread and move,
and be part of other lives too.
This mind will die,
its traces too, its records,
all in due time.
This too need not despair;
For there will be other minds
in other times.
Similar experiences, similar delights.

This existence just happened,
so too will many more.
It matters not if I'm beloved,
though it's nice and good to hear it more.

So come stranger,
tell me about yourself.
You are beloved too,
show me what burns inside of you.

Atoms

Seven billion billion billion atoms say hello.
My seven billion billion billion atoms say hi also.
All the atoms, inside and outside,
our seven billion billion billion each,
vibrate alike.

We don't see it, or feel it,
but we are exchanging a few million or billion atoms,
between our own seven billion billion billion,
as we breathe.

Some of my atoms move, and the order is paid.
I take my drink.
My seven billion billion billion atoms sip.
I still think I am me,
but my seven billion billion billion atoms would disagree.

Grace

I live, I learn, I am aware.
In Nature, this brings me despair,
anxiety for all the causes and effects
outside my reach.

In Grace, however, this means
I let go of trying to win,
to survive even, to an extent,
my drive is accepting of causes
and effects alike.

Awareness then brings beauty as is
rather than what it ought to be.
To be calm in the storm,
to see beauty in tragedy or war
though still wanting and acting
to see it gone.

In Nature its game
has nutrients as the energy
and copies as reward
no matter the cost or the expense
to achieve that goal.

In Grace I wonder
if Love is the energy.
Grace itself is fleeting
in the rare moments when I live it.
I wonder if it weakens
and leaves me to be taken advantage of.
But oh to feel it, when it comes.
All is forgiven.

Made in the USA
Columbia, SC
26 July 2021